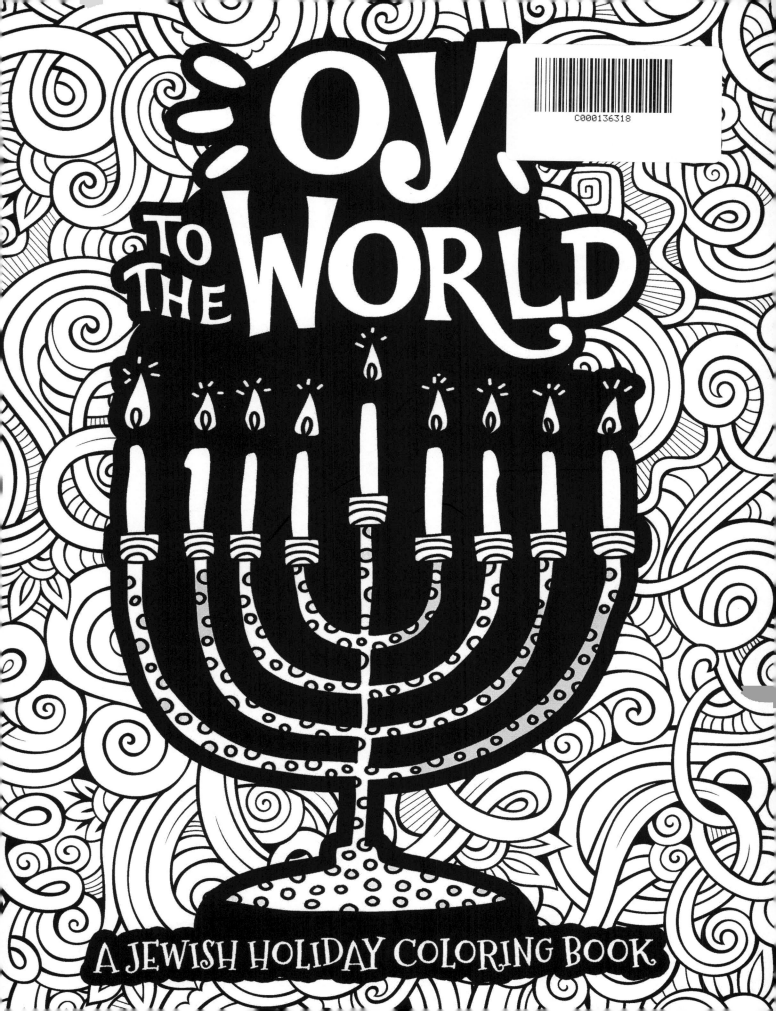

Illustrated by Micaela

ISBN-13: 978-1945888922
ISBN-10: 194588892X

FREE DOWNLOADS

35 FREE COLOURING CARDS

www.papeteriebleu.com/oyvey

YOUR DOWNLOAD CODE: HUK2399

PapeterieBleu

Papeterie Bleu

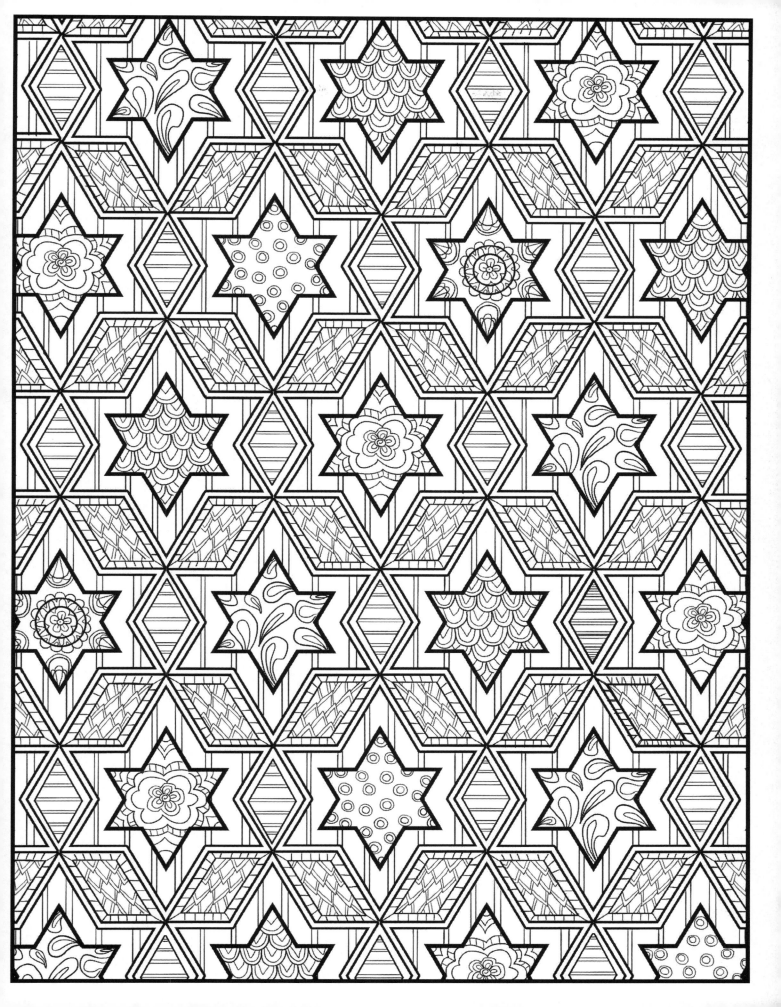

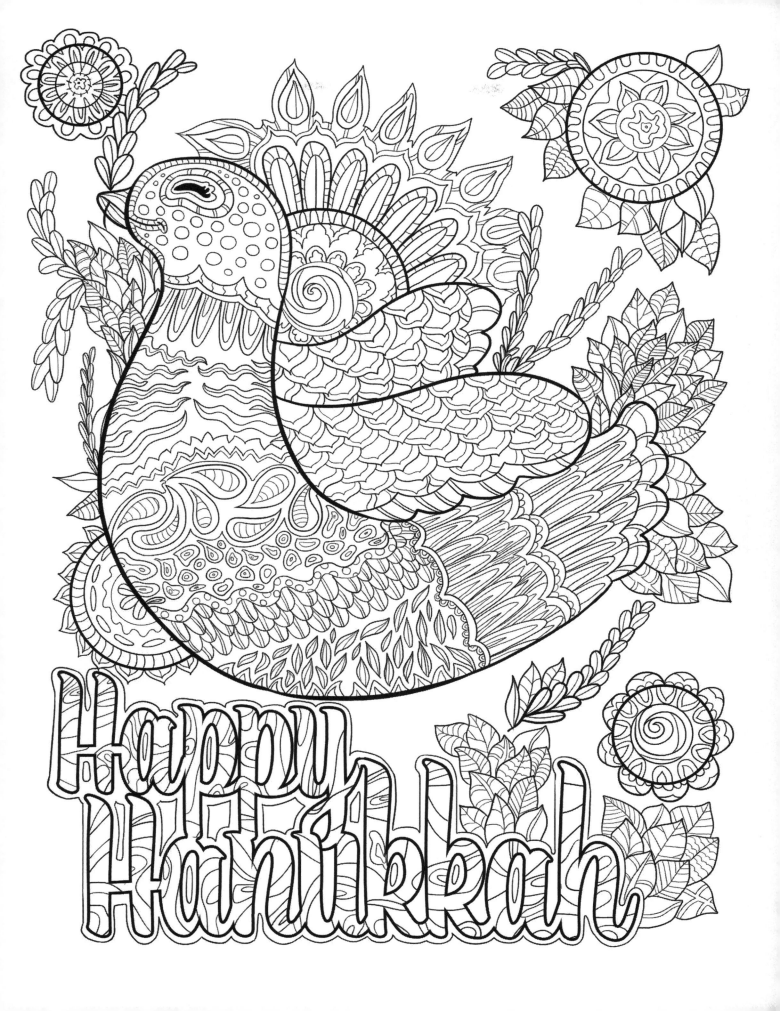

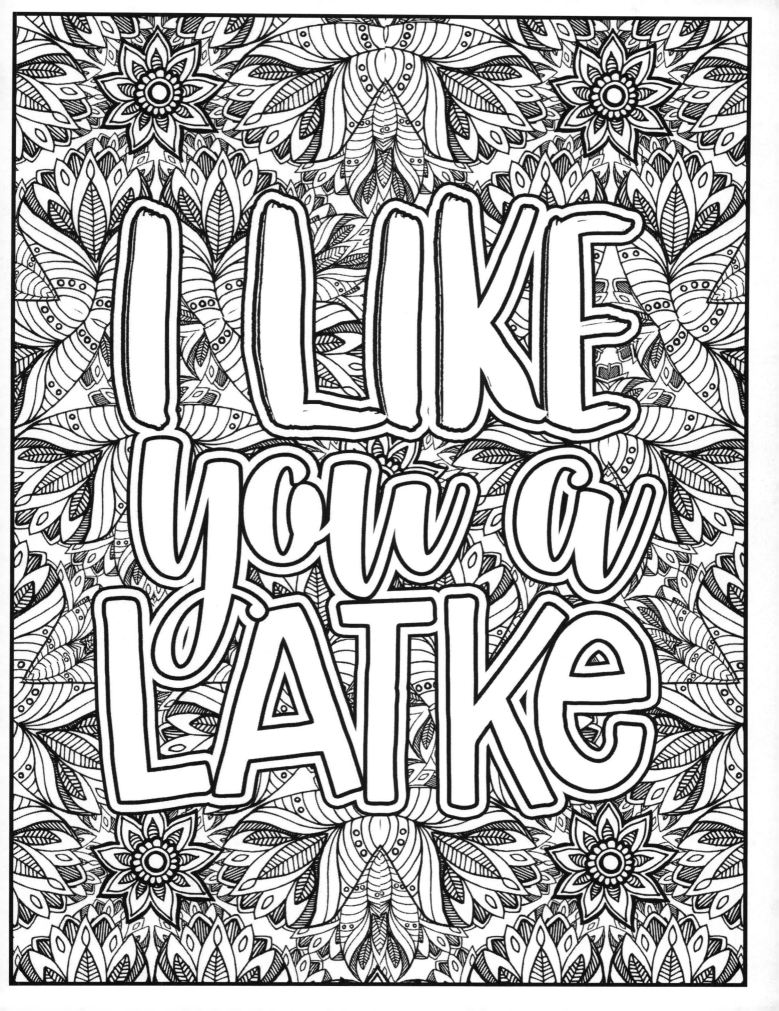

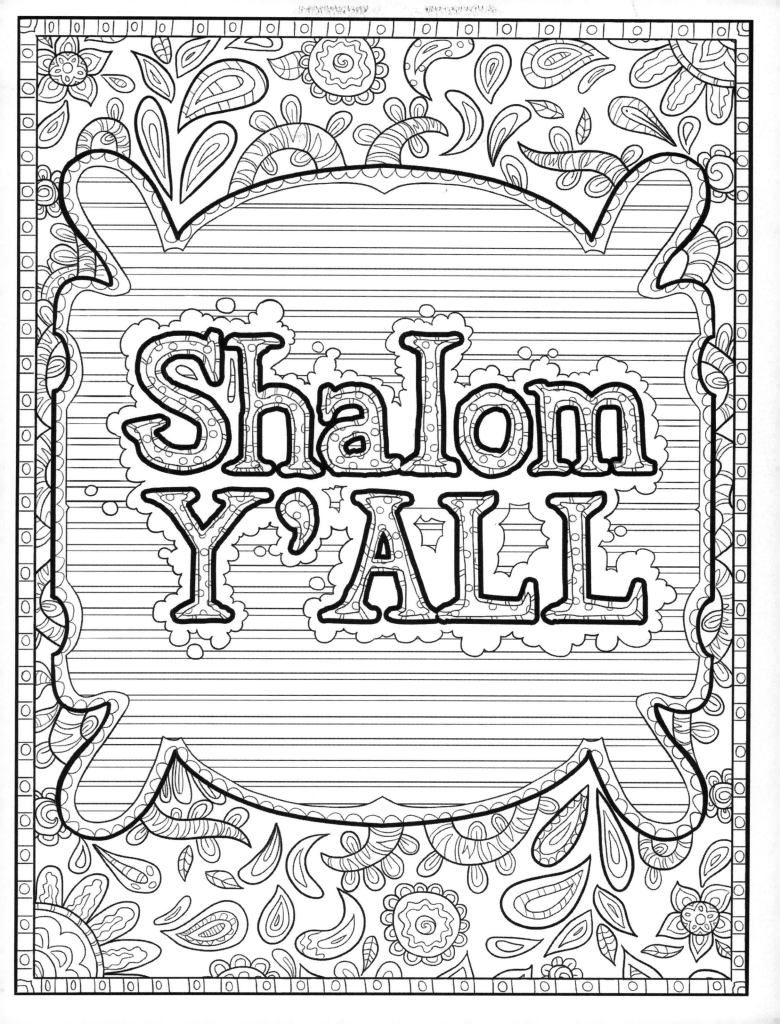

BE SURE TO FOLLOW US
ON SOCIAL MEDIA FOR THE
LATEST NEWS, SNEAK
PEEKS, & GIVEAWAYS

[Instagram icon] @PapeterieBleu

[Facebook icon] Papeterie Bleu

[Twitter icon] @PapeterieBleu

ADD YOURSELF TO OUR MONTHLY
NEWSLETTER FOR FREE DIGITAL
DOWNLOADS AND DISCOUNT CODES

www.papeteriebleu.com/newsletter

CHECK OUT OUR OTHER BOOKS!

www.papeteriebleu.com

  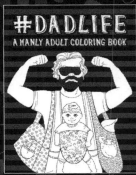 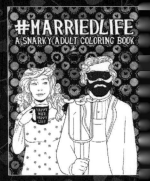 

CHECK OUT OUR OTHER BOOKS!

CHECK OUT OUR OTHER BOOKS!

www.papeteriebleu.com

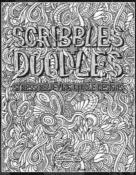

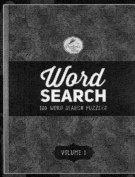

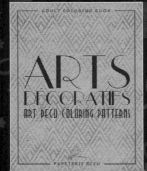
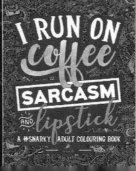

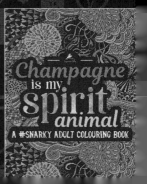

Printed in Great Britain
by Amazon